NOTTINGHAM

From Old Photographs

JOSEPH EARP

AMBERLEY

Paul Nix, founder of the Nottingham Hidden History Team.

First published 2014

Amberley Publishing
The Hill, Stroud
Gloucestershire, GL5 4EP

www.amberley-books.com

British Library Cataloguing in Publication Data.
A catalogue record for this book is available from the British Library.

ISBN 978 1 4456 3459 3 (print)
ISBN 978 1 4456 3471 5 (ebook)

Typeset in 10pt on 12pt Sabon.
Typesetting and Origination by Amberley Publishing.
Printed in the UK.

Contents

Nottingham, looking from the top of the castle.

Introduction

The City of Nottingham as we know it today began life as an Anglo-Saxon settlement. By the late nineteenth century, Nottingham had developed into a thriving city. Nottingham has seen many changes over the centuries, and many generations of Nottingham people have come and gone. These generations have, in their own way, added their mark to Nottingham. Most of Nottingham's medieval history, both visibly and archaeologically, has been lost to development and time. The great redevelopment of the city in the 1960s and '70s saw many historic areas and buildings lost to the bulldozer; areas such as Maid Marian Way, Narrow Marsh, Broad Marsh, Drury Hill and around the Castle, and buildings such as the Black Boy Hotel, the Victoria station, the Exchange Building, Collin's Almshouses, the Jasmine Cottages, the Flying Horse Hotel and even the original medieval castle, have all been lost forever. However, if you explore around the city, a large proportion of our heritage still remains. Nonetheless, this existing heritage needs to be appreciated and preserved for the future.

Through photographs and other images, *Nottingham From Old Photographs* documents and reflects the change from the early settlement of *Tigguo Cobauc* (a place of cave dwellings) to the modern city of Nottingham. Most of the photographs and research within these pages have come from the collection of the late Paul Nix of the Nottingham Hidden History Team (NHHT). The work of the Hidden History Team exceeds well over forty years of effort relating to Nottingham local history. The original NHHT was formed in 1965 to try to save, or at least record before destruction, the cave sites continually discovered during the major redevelopment of the city in the 1960s and onwards. Almost every day new sites were unearthed and destroyed before anyone was officially notified; the last thing contractors wanted was someone telling them to stop work on a project. 'Time is money', as they say.

During this period the team – about ten strong (varying on availability of members at any particular time) – recorded, cleaned and helped preserve many sites that would have been lost for ever. The team's founder was Mr Paul Nix. In the early days, the team found themselves involved with various cave explorations. Their cave highlights saw them recording Daniel in the Lion's Den and the Colonnade in the Park Terrace. They were also one of the first to record the Old Angel Inn, Judge's Restaurant on Mansfield Road, caves under Long Row, and caves under the old Flying Horse Hotel, plus many more. Perhaps the highlight of the team's work was a rescue excavation of the Goose Gate caves. By the end of the team's dig, the council's Department of Technical Services decided to save the caves and preserve them.

In the 1980s and 1990s, the team, with the help of Dr Robert Morrell and Syd Henley, conducted research and work on Nottingham's history, folklore and local archaeology. The team published quarterly magazines on their findings, but this team lapsed for a few years after the death of Paul Nix in 2008. Luckily Bob Trubshaw and Frank Earp managed to save some of the Hidden History Team's vast collection of photographs, postcards, slides and research. The result of the recover and preservation of the collection is this book.

It is hoped that the book will appeal to both the casual reader, local historians and anyone interested in the local heritage of Nottingham. There are many works that depict the history and development of Nottingham through photographs and images, and each of these has in their own way given the reader a photographic history of the early town. However, most of these books repeat the same images and are therefore 'much of a muchness'. In this respect, this book is unique. Combined with the author's own photographs and previously unpublished documents, images and photographs from the collection of the late Paul Nix, we see a new side to Nottingham's ever changing history.

Acknowledgements

First and foremost, gratitude and credit must go to Paul Nix of the Nottingham Hidden History Team. Without Paul's forty years or more of research and work on Nottingham local history, this book would never have been possible. He had the foresight to photograph, record and research Nottingham's heritage, before, in some cases, it was lost forever to development in the city.

I am indebted to Bob Trubshaw of Heart of Albion Press; special thanks must go to him for saving some of the collection of Paul Nix's and placing it into my ownership. I am also grateful for his help and advice during the preparation period for this book.

I am greatly indebted to Dorothy Ritchie and the staff of the Nottingham Local Studies Library. Thanks must go to them for their help and permission for the reproduction of certain photographs. My thanks go to John Howorth from the *Topper* newspaper and *Nottingham Post* for allowing access to their vast collection of photographs.

My gratitude goes to my parents, Frank and Lynn Earp. Their support and help throughout the preparation of this book must be acknowledged. I am also specifically thankful to my father, Frank Earp, who really inspired me to take up my interest in history and specifically Nottingham local history. Finally, I am indebted to my partner Iris, for her continued help and encouragement.

Every attempt has been made to trace and contact the original owners of all images used in this book where relevant. If copyright has inadvertently been infringed, copyright holders should write to the publishers with full details upon copyright being established. A correct credit will be incorporated into future editions of the book. The majority of the photographs used for this book have come from the Paul Nix Collection and the author's own private collection.

1

Nottingham: An Ever-Changing City

Maid Marian Way in Nottingham under construction in June 1965. By the time the photograph was taken, the new Maid Marian Way was near completion. Nottingham City Council had decided as early as 1945 that it needed a new road from the junction of Upper Parliament Street and Chapel Bar down to Canal Street. However, it would take many more years until work eventually started for the new road.

Maid Marian Way from Parliament Street, December 1964. The main reason the road was built was to relieve traffic pressure on the city centre after it started to be strangled by cars in the late 1950s. Work started in 1963, with the demolition of many historical buildings and old medieval streets to make way for the new road.

The Salutation Inn can be seen in the centre of the picture, as well as St Nicholas' Church, which is located on the far right. The image was taken from the corner of Friar Lane in 1964 during the Maid Marian Way development. Some buildings survived the demolition, such as The Salutation Inn and St Nicholas' Church, but with their frontages much reduced.

The Maid Marian Way Development in June 1965. Here can be seen the newly erected concrete office blocks, hotels and car parks that would go on to dominate the skyline of Nottingham. The building in the centre on street level would go on to become a Tesco. It was later used as the Tales of Robin Hood Museum, until that eventually closed in 2009.

The top of Friar Lane and the new Maid Marian Way during the construction works of January 1965. The road was finally completed in the same year as this image was taken. Less than two years after the road was completed, it was given a label that has stuck ever since: 'the ugliest street in Europe'.

The new subways can be seen being built in 1965. This particular subway seen here led from Friar Lane. Pedestrian subways under busy roads on the edge of city centres are a common legacy from the 1960s and '70s. The Maid Marian Way was built as an inner-city dual carriageway. The intersection with Friar Lane was turned into a roundabout with a sunken plaza, which linked four pedestrian subways each served by stairways and ramps. There are similar examples in many other UK towns and cities. The subways would later be filled in by Nottingham City Council.

The Salutation from the corner of Friar Lane in June 1965, showing the near completion of the subways. There was always mixed opinion about the subways under Maid Marian Way. Some thought that they were ugly and were too out of date for a modern Nottingham, while most were upset when they were finally filled in. A lot of people miss the convenience and safety of using the subways, which acted as a shortcut from the busy road. Perhaps the most missed feature of the subway is the newsagent stand, which was located in the central opening of the subway complex.

Friar Lane subway around 1999, just a few years before it would finally be filled in by Nottingham City Council. Some fondly remember the subways, while others regard them as run-down places to fear after nightfall. When the decision was finally made to fill in the subways, it caused a variety of reactions from the local residents of Nottingham.

The Hippodrome demolition, March 1973. The Nottingham Hippodrome was designed by the respected Theatre Architect Bertie Crewe in 1908 and opened on 28 September that year. The interior was all Georgian Revival period; there was lots of ornate gilt paint with red plush, not only on the carpets and seats, but also lining the front of the balconies and the drapes in the two-tier side boxes that augmented the classic horseshoe-shaped auditorium with three circle levels above the stalls (a dress circle, circle and the upper circle). Like so many other theatres, the Hippdrome finally closed. It was later used as The Gaumont Cinema, before it was finally demolished.

Above: The Black Boy Hotel being prepared for demolition at the end of the 1960s. The hotel began life in the seventeenth century on land owned by the Brunts family of East Bridgford, and by 1700 the inn was an established staging post with coaches departing to all parts of the country. In 1887/88 Nottingham's famous architect Watson Fothergill rebuilt the hotel. In 1897, he also extended and added to it. With its massive central tower with dark wooden gables and a Bavarian balcony, the hotel was a major landmark in Nottingham city centre. Its final demolition caused huge outcry from the local residents, which has not gone away to this day. It was replaced by a dull concrete Littlewoods store.

Left: Excavations for the Ritz Cinema, Angel Row, 1934, which was built for and originally operated by the County Cinemas chain. Local architect Albert J. Thraves was brought in by the main architects Verity & Beverley to assist with the construction. The Ritz Cinema was fully equipped with a large stage, a Conacher 4-Manual/22-Rank theatre organ and a large café/restaurant. Odeon Cinemas bought out the controlling interest of County Cinemas in 1935 and became the company's sole owners in 1939. The cinema kept its original name until 1944 when it was rebranded as an Odeon. The cinema eventually closed and the building was demolished in 2012.

Woodborough Road church during demolition in March 1973. The foundation stone for the chapel was laid on 22 May 1871. The church closed in July 1940 and was sold to Christian Scientists who remained until 1951 (when they moved to Villa Road) and the Emmanuel Full Gospel church took possession.

Broadmarsh under construction in May 1971. Broadmarsh Shopping Centre was officially opened by the Duke of Gloucester on the 25 March 1975. Part of the area of where the shopping centre now stands was once occupied by the Franciscan friary known as Greyfriars, which was dissolved in 1539. The area was heavily developed between the sixteenth and twentieth centuries. Despite its historic interest and much local opposition, all the buildings were demolished to accommodate the new shopping centre. During preparation of the site, many caves and cellars dug into the soft sandstone foundations of the city were rediscovered. The caves were to be destroyed as part of the construction, but activism from residents and historians allowed the caves to be preserved. Some are now open to the public as part of the City of Caves Museum.

Above: Site of Ashmore's shop, Hockley, in March 1970. The site was demolished to make way for the Sheriffs Way, as were many buildings and properties within the Hockley area. The area around Hockley today is known for its vibrant retail shops, bars, restaurants and pubs.

Opposite above: Hockley, March 1970. In the photograph property can be seen being removed for the Sheriffs Way development. Hockley lies adjacent to the Lace Market. With many bars, restaurants and trendy clothes shops, it is a vibrant, modern section of the city, and has been described as 'the Soho of Nottingham'. The area was originally (from around 1285) called 'Walker Gate', from the practice of 'walking' or stamping upon cloth to make it softer after weaving.

Opposite below: The site of Mount Street bus station under development, 14 July 1968. The bus station was situated between Mount Street and Park Row, and was demolished in the spring of 1968. The excavation on the adjoining car park to the site revealed a length of the old town wall.

Above: Trinity Square car park under construction. The car park was built on the site of the Holy Trinity Church, and was eventually demolished in 2005 when the whole area was redeveloped.

Opposite above: Trinity Square in September 1963. The area was the site of Holy Trinity church. The church was in the English style and was built on the site in 1839, dedicated to the Holy Trinity. It was demolished in 1958. The site was used for a multistorey car park, which can be seen under development in the photograph. The car park was demolished in 2005/06 and the area is now used for retail outlets. The site is now known as Trinity Square in remembrance to the church.

Opposite below: The demolition of the Victoria station, 1968. Some consider the demolition of the Victoria railway station as the biggest loss to Nottingham's architectural history. The station was designed by the architect Albert Edward Lambert. It was opened by the Nottingham Joint Station Committee on 24 May 1900 and closed on 4 September 1967. The station building was entirely demolished (except for the clock tower) and the Victoria Centre shopping centre was built on the site, incorporating the old station clock tower into the main entrance.

Development for the Victoria Centre, August 1971. The Victoria Centre stands on the site of the old Nottingham Victoria railway station, which was demolished in 1967/68. The clock tower and the former Victoria Station Hotel are the only parts of the old station to survive. The shopping centre was built between 1967 and 1972 by Taylor Woodrow.

2

Nottingham's Old Market Square

Nottingham's Market Place, *c.* 1806. Nottingham's Old Market Square was not the site of the original weekday market for Saxon Nottingham. This was at Weekday Cross but there was often friction when the Norman population from around the castle had to come into the Saxon town. William Peverel, builder of Nottingham Castle, founded a new market on neutral ground for the two boroughs, now known as the Old Market Square. It was a large market of 5½ acres, functioning from the eleventh century until 1928.

Nottingham's Market Place, c. 1826. It has always been reputed that the square is the largest public space in the UK after London's Trafalgar Square. The square has long been at the centre of Nottingham life. When it was first created, a wall was built across the market, running east to west, dividing the animal market from the grain and commercial market. It has long been speculated that the wall was built to separate the two peoples of the town, the English (Anglo Saxons) and the French (the Normans). The old positioning of this historic wall was reinstated when the square was redesigned in the 2000s, with a stainless-steel drainage channel down the centre of the square.

The Exchange building, Market Place, c. 1826. The building which stood in the market place was known as the 'Exchange'. It was completed in 1726 but, by 1815, it needed considerable repair and remodelling. The building was not originally constructed to act as the meeting place of the Corporation of Nottingham. The Corporation met in the original Guildhall that stood where the Nottingham Contemporary now stands at Weekday Cross. In 1877, the Corporation moved to temporary premises while the Exchange was converted to use for meetings. In 1879, the Corporation met in the Exchange for the first time, thus making the Council House site the ceremonial headquarters of Nottingham's civic government.

Above: The Old Exchange taken from
Long Row, *c.* 1896. A very quiet-looking
Nottingham Market Place can be seen in the
photograph. On market days, the market
square would be crowded with hundreds
of people going to the market for their
shopping. At the centre of the image stands
the Exchange. Between 1724 and 1726, the
Exchange was built by Marmaduke Pennell
at a cost of £2,400, and this became the
administrative offices of the council together
with the Old Guildhall in Weekday Cross.

Right: The Shambles, Old Exchange,
Nottingham, early 1900s. In the 1920s,
plans were developed to build the present
Council House and the Exchange Arcade
behind. The Exchange and the Shambles were
demolished during 1926. It was reported that
the demolition allegedly disturbed and drove
away an enormous number of rats. The rats
were seen to scurry up Friar Lane.

50. Exchange & Market Place, Nottingham

Above: Nottingham Illuminations celebrating the Coronation of 1911. The Coronation of George V took place on 22 June 1911. Celebrations for the Coronation in Nottingham included a military parade in the Market Square itself, as well as celebrations in Nottingham Forest.

Opposite above: The Shambles, Old Exchange, Nottingham, early 1900s. The Shambles that can be seen here was the meat market for Nottingham. It was located under what is now the dome of the Council House. This was an area of around forty butcher's stalls that had become considered unsanitary. It left a good deal to be desired from the hygiene point of view, for under it were caves used for storage of raw sewage and it was allegedly reported that semi-wild cats were often seen nibbling the meat before it was sold.

Opposite below: The Exchange and Market Place. The clock on the Old Exchange can be seen distinctively from a distance. A clock was presented for the Exchange by 1728 by the famous clock builder James Woolley of Codnor, and in return he was made a Burgess of Nottingham. In 1830, John Whitehurst and Son of Derby provided a new clock for the Exchange at a cost of £100. The old clock was acquired by St Nicholas' church, Nottingham and the dial from this clock is still in situ on the church tower. On 19 September 1836, a new dial was added to the clock by Shepperley for £46 and this was illuminated by a gas jet. On 26 November 1836, a fire broke out and considerable damage was caused to the building.

Above: Nottingham's Market Place, early 1900s. The arcaded walks around the square grew out of the jettied, overhanging fronts of buildings, which, when the timbers became weak, were propped up with timber posts. If no one objected to these for a year, they could be made permanent walkways. Running from Sheep Lane (Market Street) to Cow Lane (Clumber Street) was an open sewer which probably fed the pumps and wells in the square. For many centuries, there were two crosses in the square and one on The Poultry, which were the centres of activity in the early days.

Opposite above: Nottingham Market Place, *c.* 1901. Right from the medieval period to the late 1920s, a Saturday market was held in the square. Street names like The Poultry, Cheapside and Beastmarket Hill recall the use of the area as a market.

Opposite below: Market Square, *c.* 1902. Historically, the square formed a meeting place for the people of Nottingham and is also the location for local events, civic protests, royal visits, celebrations, and public mourning. A number of Nottingham's defining moments have taken place in the square.

The Market Place, taken from South Parade, 1889. South Parade is a very different area today compared with the picture. Long gone are its cobbled streets, the Exchange building and the market that can be seen to the left. Long gone are the horses and carts that once dominated the roads of the city. Today, along South Parade, horses are no longer the dominating source of transport, instead a modern tram can constantly be seen travelling along its route.

Above: Nottingham's new Council House under construction, *c.* 1927. The Council House was built between 1927 and 1929. It replaced the old Exchange building after that was demolished in 1926. The contractor for the demolition of the Exchange was Greenham Ltd of London. When it was announced that the old Exchange would be demolished to make way for a new civic building, the local residents strongly objected as they thought the demolition was a great shame.

Right: The dome of the new Nottingham Council House under construction, *c.* 1927. One of the building's most striking features is definitely the great dome. This rises 200 feet above ground level and is visible for miles. The dome houses the chiming clock and Little John, a 10½-ton striking bell that is reputed to have the deepest tone in the country.

The Council House, Nottingham, near to its completion, c. 1927. The Council House was designed by Thomas Cecil Howitt. It was built in the Neo-Baroque style, characterised by the huge pillars that circle the building along with the carvings on the façade. The building was officially opened by HRH the Prince of Wales (later King Edward VIII and the Duke of Windsor) on 22 May 1929.

The newly built Nottingham Old Market Square and Council House, c. 1930s. When the new Council House was built, the market, which had been in the square since at least the eleventh century, was relocated to the site of old St John's prison on King Edward Street, and now has moved to the Victoria Shopping Centre. As well as the market moving, the Nottingham Goose Fair was also relocated. The Market Square was the setting of the Goose Fair, an annual fair originating over 700 years ago. The Goose Fair was moved in 1928 to the Forest Recreation Ground.

THE COUNCIL HOUSE, NOTTINGHAM

Above: Nottingham Old Market Square and Council House, *c.* 1950s. The Council House is constructed of Portland stone from the same quarry used by Christopher Wren for St Paul's Cathedral. The terrace overlooking the Old Market Square has eight massive columns, above are twenty-one figures representing the activities of the council, also modelled by Joseph Else, principal of the Nottingham School of Art. The frieze behind depicts traditional local crafts such as bell founding, mining and alabaster carving.

Right: South Parade, Old Market Square. South Parade in the Market Square was formerly known as Timber Hill. There was a row of seven elm trees which stretched across the market parallel to South Parade, which were said to be 'rather famous because of their handsome appearance'. Against them were stored the great baulks of timber and the planks that were brought to Nottingham Market Place for sale, and consequently South Parade got its ancient name of Timber Hill.

Above: Crowds gather in Nottingham's market place for Armistice Day, 11 November 1922. This Armistice Day would have been one of the first held in Nottingham. The very first one was held in Buckingham Palace, to mark the armistice signed between the Allies and Germany at the end of the First World War.

Opposite above: The junction of Beastmarket Hill and Long Row, Market Square, *c.* 1950s. The road leading off to the top is Market Street. At the top of Market Street can be seen the Theatre Royal. Market Street started out as a narrow alley called Sheep Lane but due to its limited width quite a few accidents happened, pedestrians going up met with carts coming down, causing people to be squashed against the sides – usually resulting in bloodstains on the floor and wall. This led to the locals referring to it as 'Blood Lane'. It was later renamed Market Street in 1866 following 'civic improvements' around the square.

Opposite below: Nottingham's 'Left Lion', 2011. Two large stone lions guard the Council House steps. These lions have become a famous meeting point for many decades for thousands of Nottingham residents. The 'Left Lion' in particular has long since been adopted by locals as a meeting place. There are alternative names attached to them, some people call them 'Menelaus' and 'Agamemnon'. Other names that have been given to them are Leo and Oscar. Many of Nottingham's residents over the years, when planning a meeting point in the city, have used the expression 'meet you by the lions'. This saying in itself has subsequently become part of the local dialect of the city.

General View of the Market Place.

Above: Royal visit to Nottingham, 24 June 1914. As well as visiting Nottingham's Market Place, King George V also visited the forest, with thousands of cheering crowds who greeted him and the Queen. It is interesting to note that the king visited Nottingham just weeks before the start of the First World War.

Opposite above: Armistice Day Parade in the Market Square, 1966. The Lord Mayor of Nottingham, Percy Holland, can be seen to the left of the picture. Armistice Day (which coincides with Remembrance Day and Veterans Day) is commemorated every year on 11 November to mark the armistice signed between the Allies of the First World War and Germany at Compiègne, France. The armistice took effect at eleven o'clock in the morning – the eleventh hour of the eleventh day of the eleventh month of 1918.

Opposite below: Guard of Honour in front of the Old Exchange. The Guard of Honour can be seen awaiting the arrival of the Prince of Wales in the Nottingham Market Place, 1 August 1923.

Left: Gen. Dwight D. Eisenhower acknowledges the cheers from the Council House. Eisenhower can be seen waving from the balcony of the Council House on 26 October 1945. On the day of his visit, most schools in Nottinghamshire were granted a half-day holiday.

Below: May Day Demonstration, 5 May 1968. The demonstration shown here was a protest against the war in Vietnam. The Old Market Square has for hundreds of years been a platform for a number of demonstrations and protests. Not all protests in the Square have been peaceful. Perhaps the most well-known and even violent protests were the Luddite movement, which began in March 1811, and Reform Bill of 1831. Both the Luddite movement and the Reform Bill situation started as protests, but ended in violent riots.

Right: One of the original fountains in the Old Market Square, October 2001. Since the 1927 design of the square, there have been water fountains present. Two fountains flanked the central procession and were in the centre of individual square pools. These remained until the redesign by Kathryn Gustafson (and associates) in 2007, when a new fountain and water feature were added towards the top end of the square.

Below: Christmas in the Old Market Square, 1999. Cars can still be seen on both sides of the square. This photograph was taken a few years before the redesign of the square and before it became pedestrianised along Long Row.

The Old Market Square, October 2001. The square was redesigned in 2004 and finally completed in March 2007. Many local residents of Nottingham often comment about the great loss of some of the old features of the square before its redesign, such as the individual fountains, trees and many of the benches that were spread around the square. One of the biggest features missed by the residents is the toilets, which were located underground within the Market Square.

Work being carried out for the new redesign of the Market Square, 2006. The square was redesigned by Kathryn Gustafson (and associates) in 2004 and completed in March 2007. The final slab prior to the reopening was laid by the Lord Mayor and Mrs Elizabeth Strongman. The new square is a single tier area, including the recreation of an ancient border which once divided Nottingham. A new water feature dominates the west side of the square, with jet fountains and waterfalls.

3

Nottingham Castle

A view of Nottingham Castle from the north-east. This is one of the earliest images of Nottingham Castle. It depicts what Nottingham Castle might have looked like in the sixteenth century. It was published by Geo Simons and included in James Orange's *History of Nottingham, Vol. 2* and engraved by J. Bache.

NOTTINGHAM CASTLE.

G 5821

Above: A painting by Henry Thomas Dawson showing Charles I raising his standard outside Nottingham Castle's walls, beginning the English Civil War. By the early 1600s, Nottingham Castle had ceased to be a royal residence and was already in a semi-ruined state. Ironically, for most of the war the site was held by the opposing Parliamentary forces under the command of Col. Hutchinson. Hutchinson and his men repulsed several Royalist attacks, and they were the last group to hold the castle. After the execution of Charles I in 1649, the castle was razed to prevent its reuse.

Opposite above: A Victorian reconstruction of the likely appearance of Nottingham Castle in the late medieval period. In 1067/68, William the Conqueror ordered for a motte and bailey castle to be built upon a high ridge, which is now known as Castle Rock. Castle Rock provided an easily defensible site commanding the crossing of the River Trent that linked the main road between London and the North. In the twelfth century the castle was rebuilt in stone by Henry II. It became one of the principal royal fortresses in the country right up until the sixteenth century.

Opposite below: The seventeenth-century Ducal Mansion, early 1900s. After the restoration of Charles II in 1660, the present Ducal Mansion was built by Henry Cavendish, 2nd Duke of Newcastle between 1674 and 1679 on the foundations of the medieval castle. Cavendish would not survive to see his mansion finished, his son would go on to complete the work.

Nottingham Castle, early 1900s. The mason for the Ducal Mansion was Samuel Marsh of Lincoln, who also worked for the Duke at Bolsover Castle. His designs are generally thought to have been strongly influenced by Rubens's published engravings of the Palazzi di Genova. The Duke's mansion is a rare surviving example in England of Artisan Mannerist architecture. Although the modern Ducal Mansion is a fine example of seventeenth-century architecture, the removing of the original medieval castle was a great loss of an important example of medieval architecture in England.

The castle positioned high on top of the Castle Rock, looking up from the bottom. It is very clear why the Castle Rock site was chosen to build a castle. With cliffs 130 feet (40 metre) high to the south and west, it is a prominent feature in the landscape.

Reform rioters watch Nottingham Castle burn, 8 October 1831. On the evening of 8 October 1831, conviviality ruled in Nottingham. It was Goose Fair time and thousands thronged into the Old Market Square, but the jubilant mood quickly darkened the following morning with the arrival of the London mail coach. The Reform Bill had been rejected by the House of Lords and angry Nottingham citizens fixed their sights on specific targets. The highest profile target of the 1831 riots was Nottingham Castle. In protest against the Duke of Newcastle's opposition to the Reform Act 1832, they burnt down his Ducal Mansion.

The castle from the Meadows prior to restoration showing Park Terrace, 1870. After the burning of the Castle in 1831, it remained an empty and derelict shell for nearly fifty years. It was restored in 1875 by Thomas Chambers Hine, and opened in 1878 by the Prince of Wales (later King Edward VII) as the Nottingham Castle Museum and Art Gallery.

Nottingham Castle gatehouse, *c.* 1900. The gatehouse before its 1908 restoration. The gatehouse was the only external gate into the medieval castle. The gatehouse was built between 1250 and 1255 and stood two storeys high with a thick, timber door, a portcullis and a drawbridge. The thirteenth-century masonry from the gatehouse survives to the lower string course, covered by twentieth-century ashlar cladding. Today, only the gatehouse, outer walls and caves below give a hint of the traditional castle visitors often expect to find.

The Long Gallery, a few years after it had opened in 1878. The Long Gallery houses a permanent display of the best of the museum's fine art. The painting collection covers British and European art ranging in date from the eleventh century to the present day. Today, Nottingham Castle is a popular visitor attraction and is Nottingham's main museum and art gallery. It houses most of the City of Nottingham's fine and decorative art collections, galleries on the history and archaeology of Nottingham and the surrounding areas, and the regimental museum of the Sherwood Foresters.

4

Buildings & Architecture

PRESENTED BY
JOHN MANNING ESQ. MAYOR,
To *Miss Charlotte Mather*
ON THE OCCASION OF THE OPENING OF THE
NEW TRENT BRIDGE,
NOTTINGHAM, JULY 25 TH. 1871.

An invitation from the Lord Mayor John Manning to the official opening of the new Trent Bridge on 25 July 1871. There has been a bridge on the Trent at Nottingham since at least 920, which was known as the 'Hethbeth Bridge'. A second bridge was constructed in the twelfth century, and in the sixteenth century the responsibility for the upkeep and repair of the bridge passed to Nottingham Corporation. By the nineteenth century, the old medieval Trent Bridge was worn and became increasingly dangerous to use. It was decided that a new one would be designed and erected next to the old bridge. A couple of arches from the old Trent Bridge are still preserved on the south bank of the river near the crossing.

Trent Bridge, 1920s. The current Trent Bridge was designed by architect Marriott Ogle Tarbotton. Construction started in 1868 and was completed in 1871 by Derbyshire iron maker, Andrew Handyside. The general contractor was Benton and Woodiwiss of Derby. It was completed for a cost of £30,000.

Above: The Victoria Embankment War Memorial. The memorial was completed in 1927 by T. Wallis Gordon. It is built from Portland stone ashlar, with wrought-iron gates, in a Classical Revival style, and is a tripartite triumphal arch with giant Doric columns and inscribed frieze. There are three pairs of wrought-iron gates of outstanding quality. On each side of the memorial there are curved colonnades with intermediate pedestals. Beyond this there are wrought-iron railings, 10 metres long, on plinths.

Opposite above: Boots store on Pelham Street, 26 September 1972. The photograph was taken the same year the old Boots store closed its doors for the final time. This beautiful Edwardian building was designed by architect A. N. Bromley in 1904. It stands on Pelham Street, and was Jesse Boot's flagship department store in Nottingham and the forerunner of all Boots larger stores. It included a café and even a library, along with the usual toiletry, chemist and gift departments. The Boots shop closed in 1972 and the building has since been used by a succession of other shops.

Opposite below: Theatre Square, Upper Parliament Street, *c.* 1900. The Theatre Royal can be seen to the left with the column front. The building to the adjacent right was The Empire Theatre of Varieties. The new Theatre Royal was completed in 1865 by C. J. Phipps at the cost of £15,000. C. J. Phipps would go on to become one of Victorian Britain's leading theatre designers. The Classic façade and Corinthian columns still dominate Nottingham's city centre skyline. The Empire Theatre of Varieties opened alongside in 1898 on the site of the Theatre Royal's old dressing rooms.

47

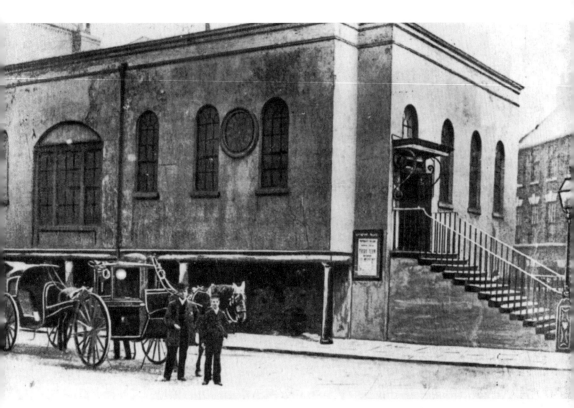

Above: Nottingham Town Hall, High Pavement, the Lace Market, 1894. The building was used as a court house and town hall. By the eighteenth century, the town had growing prosperity and an increasing administrative workload. Consequently, in 1722, the corporation decided to build a new town hall in the Market Place, and this building became known as the Exchange. The growth in municipal business in the 1870s meant that the old town hall was no longer adequate for the Corporation's use. A new Guildhall was opened in Burton Street. The old town hall was abandoned by the Corporation in 1877. The Great Central Railway bought the site in 1894 for £70 and demolished the building the following year to make way for the railway line from Victoria station, which emerged from a tunnel at Weekday Cross.

Opposite above: Interior of the Theatre Royal, 22 February 1977. The photograph was taken just one year before it was reopened in 1978. By the late 1960s, the Theatre Royal had become run down and had a reputation for poor backstage conditions. In 1969, the City Council bought it and set about restoring the theatre to its former glory. In 1978, the Theatre Royal reopened, boasting elegant and airy foyers and bars. A 1,186-seater auditorium was beautifully restored in Victorian-style green and gilt decor and with fully comprehensive and technically upgraded backstage facilities. It was officially reopened 6 June 1978 by Princess Anne who was 'impressed and delighted'. She was reported to have said on the day of reopening 'what an improvement on the old place'.

Opposite below: Adam's Lace Factory, Stoney Street, in the Lace Market, 1855. The building opened on 10 July 1855, and was designed by local architect Thomas Chambers Hine. It was extended in stages over twenty years (1854–74) as a lace warehouse and salesroom, and named after Thomas Adams himself. Adams came to Nottingham in 1830, and was a major contributor to the improvement of lace working conditions. His building had airy, open rooms, a library, classroom and even a chapel. The Adams Building was beautifully restored with support from Heritage Lottery and European grants, and officially reopened by HRH Prince Charles in February 1999.

Above: The 'Severns' building on Castle Road, 2011. Severns is one of the only few surviving medieval buildings in Nottingham. It was built in the mid-fourteenth century and originally stood on the south side of Middle Pavement (to the east entrance to the Broadmarsh Centre). Between 1969 and 1970, the building was dismantled and moved to Castle Road. It was later used as the Nottingham Lace Centre. The Lace Centre closed in 2009 and the building was sold in 2013 by Nottingham City Council.

Opposite above: The old Shire Hall on High Pavement, the Lace Market. There has been a court of justice on this site since at least the late fourteenth century. The present building was rebuilt between 1769 and 1770 by the architect James Gandon. Nikolaus Pevsner in his book, *The Buildings of Nottinghamshire*, describes the building as 'small and not especially distinguished, though in the good taste of the age. The simplified front with attached Ionic portico and an ample expanse of bare wall shows the influence of French neoclassicism. The façade and the grand jury room are all that survive from 1769–70. The Italianate extensions and the centre of the building inside are by T. C. Hine, 1876–9'. The building is now used as the Galleries of Justice Museum.

Opposite below: The Guildhall on Burton Street, late 1800s. The Guildhall was built in 1887/88 by Verity and Hunt in French Renaissance style, at a cost of £65,000. In 1996, all magistrates were moved to the new Nottingham Magistrates' Court building. Between 1996 and 2010, the Guildhall was occupied by Nottingham City Council. In 2010, the Council left for new, modern offices at Loxley House, close to Nottingham railway station. In 2013, the building was sold off by Nottingham City Council.

Seventeenth-century cottages, Brewhouse Yard, 2013. Sometimes referred to as the 'Castle Rock Cottages', they were built at the end of the 1600s. In 1977, they were restored and converted to house the Museum of Nottingham Life. There have been buildings on the 2-acre site known as Brewhouse Yard since at least the thirteenth century, when it is first mentioned in royal papers from the reign of Henry III. This mention refers to repairs to mills, which indicate, first, royal ownership and, second, that water from the River Leen, which, in a considerable feat of engineering for the time, was diverted at Lenton to provide water for both town and castle.

The Old General Hospital, 2012. In 1781/82, the building of Nottingham's first purpose-built hospital was erected. The building, in the style of a grand Italian mansion, was designed by architect John Simpson. Built of brick with string courses of stone, it was raised to the height of three storeys, with provisions for further levels to be added as and when needed. The magnificent frontage was enhanced with a large clock. To one side, a colonnaded terrace walkway led to a chapel to the rear of the building. The whole building was set in 2 acres of gardens, which included a fountain.

The Children's Hospital, Mapperley Park, c. 1908. Nottingham Children's Hospital was founded as a charitable institution in 1869 by public subscription, with the aim of providing 'for the reception, maintenance and medical treatment of children of the poor under ten years of age'. Its official title was the Free Hospital for Sick Children, but it was also known as 'St Lucy's', as the first nursing staff were recruited from the Sisters of St Lucy.

University College, Nottingham.

Above: School of Art, Nottingham, *c.* 1904. The fine-looking building on Waverley Street was built by Frederick Bakewell in 1863–65. The college was one of the first purpose-built art colleges in England and is now part of Nottingham Trent University. The building is now known as the Waverley Building.

Previous page: The old University College on Shakespeare Street, early 1900s. It first opened in 1881, closed two years later because of structural defects and reopened in 1890. When it was originally opened, it incorporated the public library, University College, technical and trade schools and the Natural History Museum. University College underwent significant expansion in the 1920s when it moved from the centre of Nottingham to a large campus on the city's outskirts. The building would be later used as the Trent Polytechnic and more recently the building is used by Nottingham Trent University. Part of the building was heavily damaged on 8/9 May 1941 by Hermann Goering's Luftwaffe.

The Albert Hall, Nottingham. In the early
1870s, the Good Templars were looking for
a site for a Nottingham Temperance Hall. Mr
Watson Fothergill, the famous local architect,
won the commission to design and build it.
The foundation stone was laid in September
1873, but funding ran out and the future of the
building looked bleak. A rescue bid was put
together with the formation of a limited liability
company. Work resumed on what was to
become the Albert Hall, costing some £14,000.
The Albert Hall was the city's largest concert
hall and a major venue for political rallies.

Fire sweeping through the Albert Hall, 22 April
1906. By the start of the twentieth century,
it was quite clear that the building could not
generate enough cash for its upkeep. Fortunately,
the Wesleyans were at this time seeking big
city venues for their great central missions. The
Albert Hall came on the market in 1901 and was
purchased by a syndicate of local businessmen
for £8,450, and opened as a mission in
September 1902. Fire swept through the hall
in April 1906, destroying Fothergill's original
building. After the fire, the hall was rebuilt in
1906–09 by A. E. Lambert. Nottingham City
Council purchased and restored the Albert Hall
in 1987.

Left: A timber-framed house, Red Lion Street, Narrow Marsh, *c.* 1919. The Narrow Marsh area became notorious in the early twentieth century for its crime, poverty and slums. This whole area was demolished in the late 1920s and early '30s. All the houses were replaced by some of the first purpose-built council houses. The timber-framed house in the photograph looks to be possibly Tudor. If these buildings were still standing today, they would undoubtedly be listed.

Below: House of Correction, Nottingham, *c.* 1895. The House of Correction was located at the east corner of Glasshouse Street and King Edward Street. It was originally a two-roomed building in 1615. An extension was completed in 1806, but it took another thirty years before new premises were completed. It took a further ten years before it complied with the Prison Reform Act and it became the town's common gaol. The prison became so overcrowded that when the Home Office took over the running of prisons in 1879 it should have been closed, but instead this was deferred until 1882 when the decision was made to build a new prison at Bagthorpe. Nottingham Gaol and the House of Correction were demolished in 1891.

5

Public Houses

Ye Olde Trip to Jerusalem, early 1900s. Ye Olde Trip to Jerusalem in Nottingham proudly states the claim to be the oldest inn in the world; the painted sign outside dates the inn from around AD 1189. The pub is said to have taken its name from the Crusades in the Holy Land led by Richard the Lionheart. Richard and his men supposedly stopped here for refreshments before they left. There is no written documentation proving the pub's origin, and the it had a completely different name over 200 years ago.

STAR CHAMBER TRIP TO JERUSALEM INN, NOTTINGHAM.

G.80

Above: The Star Chamber in the Ye Olde Trip to Jerusalem. This room is a bar which along with many other side rooms has been cut into the side of the Castle Rock. Above the bar in the photograph can be seen 'The Cursed Galleon'. The tale goes that the last three people who cleaned it are said to have died mysteriously and unexpectedly within twelve months of doing so. No one since has dared to clean the galleon because of the alleged curse.

Left: Brewing the famous Nottingham Ale. Nottingham has always been famous for its ale. It is so famous that in 1752 a ballad was written about the famous liquor. The ballad is entitled 'Nottingham Ale Boys'. The song has been speculated to have been written by an officer of the navy, simply referred to as 'Gunthorpe'. It is said he wrote the song in praise of a barrel of Nottingham ale, which had been sent to him by his brother, who kept the Punch Bowl, which was located in Peck Lane in Nottingham.

Above: Ye Olde Salutaion Inn, 1930s. The Salutation Inn, at the corner of Hounds Gate, is known to many a local as a comfortable old-style public house. The pub supposedly dates to around AD 1240. Research has suggested that the first building on the site of the pub was a homestead of an unnamed Tanner who made animal skins into leather. During the English Civil War (1642–46) both factions established recruiting rooms in the inn.

Right: The Gate Hangs Well Public House, *c.* 1900. This pub was originally located on the corner of Brewhouse Yard and was the next-door neighbour to the Ye Olde Trip to Jerusalem. It was eventually closed around 1905 and the building was demolished.

Above: The Flying Horse Hotel, 1960s. The inn was established in the 1480s. In 1799, it was known as The Traveller's Inn, and in 1813, a great dinner was held within its walls to celebrate the victories over Napoleon. To make merry, a figure of Napoleon had been brought up from London on the top of a coach, which was duly burnt in the Nottingham Market Place amid scenes of great excitement and rejoicing. The inn survived as a public house until 1989, when it was converted into a shop.

Opposite above: A rather charming photograph showing the Bell Inn on Friar Lane dating to around the early 1900s. The proprietor is listed as J. Jackson on the frontage of the pub. This was a Mr Joseph Jackson who brought the inn on 21 October 1898 for £12,500. In 1276, a Carmelite Friary was established on what is now Friar Lane with lands that included a guesthouse on the site of what is now The Bell Inn. The inn was originally constructed around 1420 (according to dendrochronological dating of timbers) as a refectory for the monks.

Opposite below: The Black Boy Hotel on Long Row, 1920s. The 1960s demolition of the Black Boy Hotel was one of Nottingham's biggest architectural disasters and also a great loss of one of Fothergill's finest buildings.

Above: Talbot Inn on Long Row, *c.* 1850. Thomas Cooper Moore's painting shows the original Talbot, which was demolished. A new Talbot opened in 1876, with the façade that can be seen today. It was sold at auction in 1929 to Yates' Wine Lodge. The inscription on the gable to Yates says that the Talbot was established in 1380. The original Talbot Inn was used by the Talbot family when they had business in the city. This family later became the Earls of Shrewsbury.

Left:: The Coach & Horses on Upper Parliament Street, *c.* 1903. A Dutch-style building with gable and decorated aedicule and pedimental arch around the door. The Express Buildings can be seen to the far right of the image and Black Boy Yard to the right of the Coach & Horses.

6

Local Industry & Transport

Queen Elizabeth II visiting the Birkin Lacemaking Company. Queen Elizabeth can be seen visiting and inspecting Nottingham lace at the lacemaking firm in July 1955. It was the Queen's first visit to Nottingham since the Coronation. Nottingham lace was and is famous worldwide.

A nineteenth-century sample of lace made in Nottingham. Lace was a symbol of high fashion and style in clothing and in the home. Two key inventions originating from Nottinghamshire gave rise to the thriving local industry. In 1589, local inventor, William Lee, developed a framework knitting machine, which enabled the manufacture of large volumes of lace. In 1808, John Heathcoate developed a hand-operated machine, which marked the beginning of the local lace industry.

OKTIS SHIELDS

When you are on a holiday you naturally desire freedom from all dress worries. At the seaside, in the country, or wherever you may spend your summer vacation, you want facility of movement and thorough ease.

Nothing annoys a woman so much as the snapping of a corset steel as the result of a little extra exertion. The OKTIS prevents all this and DOUBLES THE LIFE OF YOUR CORSET; and it cannot possibly rust your underclothing, as it contains Rustless Zalroid Stiffeners. You can obtain it from

GRIFFIN & SPALDING Ltd.,

Long Row and Market Street, NOTTINGHAM.

An advertisement for 'Oktis Shields' from Griffin & Spalding, who were located on Long Row and Market Street in Nottingham. The Griffin & Spalding department store was always very popular in the city. The store was founded in 1846 and by 1886 they had moved into a new building on the corner of Market Street. The store was later rebuilt in Portland stone in the 1920s.

Jesse Boot was a great benefactor to the City of Nottingham. He was presented with the Freedom of the City on 26 October 1920. Jesse Boot can be seen in the centre of the photograph receiving the honour. Boots has its roots in the mid-nineteenth century when John Boot, an agricultural worker, moved to Nottingham to start a new business. He opened a small herbalist store on Goose Gate in 1849. After John's death in 1860, his widow, Mary, continued trading, with the help of her young son, Jesse, who became a full partner when he was twenty-one. The store continued to flourish, and, in 1877, Jesse took sole control.

Midland Railway station, Carrington Street, Nottingham, c. 1840. The Nottingham Carrington Street railway station was the first railway station in Nottingham. It was opened in 1840 by the Midland Counties Railway. Initially, there were two lines with a central platform.

Left: Nottingham Victoria station, early 1900s, which opened on 24 May 1900, over a year after the start of main line services from London to Sheffield were passing through it. The construction was on a grand scale – around 700,000 cubic yards of sandstone rock was excavated from its cavernous site. Some 1,300 houses and twenty-four public houses previously on the site had to be demolished. The site was approximately 13 acres big and 650 yards long from north to south. It had an average width of 110 yards with a tunnel at each end of it for access.

Below: The first electric tram in Nottingham leaving from Sherwood to Nottingham's Market Place, 1 January 1901. The ride cost 2*d*. Demand for the service was so great that more trams were put on to cope, increasing the five-minute service to every three minutes at peak times.

A large crowd gathering together for the last tram in Nottingham, *c.* 1936. The 190 tram pulled into its city centre depot for the last time in 1936. The first tram routes, which were horse-pulled trams, opened in Nottingham on 17 September 1878. Gradually routes were replaced by trolleybuses, or motorbuses, until in 1936 only the Mapperley and Arnold routes remained. The Mapperley route changed to motorbuses on 2 February and on 6 September; the same thing happened on the Arnold route, marking the end of the first generation of trams in Nottingham.

Above: Windmills by the forest, mid-1800s. The windmills that once stood on the ridge of the forest were nearly all post-mills, of wooden construction, comparatively easy to dismantle and cart to another site. Some were brought in from elsewhere; some were moved away so the numbers could change over time. When the forest ridge was made part of the allotted recreation ground by the 1845 Enclosure Act, all the windmills had to be removed, except the only one built of brick, which was on the other side of the road on private land. At that time there were thirteen mills on the ridge.

Left: Whitehalls tenement factory. On 5 August 1905, Whitehalls tenement factory on Wollaton Street was destroyed by fire.

7

Public Open Spaces,
Cemeteries & Churches

Nottingham Arboretum, showing the lake to the left of the photograph and the aviary on the right. This scene has not changed at all since the arboretum was opened on 11 May 1852. The aviary has always been very popular to the many thousands of visitors who have walked through the arboretum over the years. When it was first opened, the bird collection comprised hundreds of species, including an African finch and a Zebra finch from Australia. The famous cockatoo, imaginatively named Cocky by the people of Nottingham, arrived in the early days. He lived until the grand old age of 114 and reportedly died around 1968.

Above: Nottingham Arboretum, early 1900s. As Nottingham's oldest public park, the arboretum was developed following the passing of the Nottingham Enclosure Act of 1845, which instigated the enclosure of fields and meadows that were used by the burgesses and freeholders of Nottingham to graze their animals. To compensate for the loss of public open space, the Nottingham Enclosure Act provided for a series of places of public recreation and public walks around the town. Designed by Samuel Curtis, a prominent botanist and horticultural expert, the arboretum was set within a landscape planted with trees and ornamental shrubs.

Opposite above: The Refreshment Rooms at the arboretum, Nottingham. One of the main features of the Nottingham Arboretum was the building originally designed as the Arboretum's Refreshment Rooms. Situated on the north side of the arboretum, it had commanding views over the park. As well as being a place for visitors to enjoy afternoon tea and other refreshments, the building was a popular venue for local organisations to hold annual dinners and special events such as dances, concerts and flower shows.

Opposite below: The Chinese Bell, Nottingham Arboretum, *c.* 1902. The Chinese Bell Tower was designed in 1857 by Marriott Ogle Tarbotton as a war memorial and built in 1862. The bell was looted by British troops from a temple in Canton during the Anglo-Chinese war (Opium War) of 1857–61. Two of the cannons were captured at Sebastopol in 1854–55, during the Crimean War, the other two are replicas. In 1956, the pagoda was partly demolished and the bell was moved to the regimental museum in Preston.

CHINESE BELL, ARBORETUM, NOTTINGHAM.

Above: A busy scene at the Forest Recreation Ground in Nottingham, early 1900s. Judging by the amount of people and the number of sun hats in the picture, the photograph was taken on a warm sunny day. The name 'forest' derives from medieval times when the land that is now the Forest Recreation Ground was part of Sherwood Forest, which once extended from the city of Nottingham to the north of Nottinghamshire.

Opposite above: A view of some of the long public walkways that are located throughout the Forest Recreation Ground. Leading gardener and architect of the nineteenth century Joseph Paxton was responsible for the crisscross formation of the long walkways in the Forest. The 1845 Nottingham Enclosure Act saw the site of the forest becoming one of the first original areas to be protected in perpetuity by the Act. Some 80 acres of Sherwood Forest were set aside for public recreational use.

Opposite below: Entrance to the Forest Recreation Ground looking from Forest Road East. This scene of one of the entrances to the Forest has not changed since it was first built. This area was previously known as 'the Lings' and formed the southern tip of Sherwood Forest. In the eighteenth and nineteenth centuries it was home to horse racing as well as cricket, and in 1865 Nottingham Forest Football Club practised and played here. In 1928, Goose Fair moved from its location in the Old Market Square to the Forest.

FOREST ENTRANCE — NOTTINGHAM.

The Lodge, Forest Recreation Ground, *c.* 1905. The lodge located on Mansfield Road, Nottingham, now stands at the entrance to the Forest Recreation Ground. It was built in 1857 as the lodge to the original racecourse. The Forest was once home to Nottingham's racecourse before it moved to its current location at Colwick, south-east of Nottingham.

Queen's Walk and Midland Station, Nottingham.

Queen's Walk and the Midland station, Nottingham, early 1900s. The route of Queen's Walk possibly follows an ancient pathway that ran from the River Trent ferry crossing at Wilford into the centre of Nottingham. The path was laid out formally in 1850 and named Queen's Walk in commemoration of Queen Victoria's visit to Nottingham in 1843.

The entrance to Robin Hood Chase, Nottingham, c. 1905. Robin Hood's Chase along with Queen's Walk, the arboretum, the Forest and castle grounds, developed as a public leisure space promenade after the 1845 Enclosure Act. It was created to provide leisure interests for the working classes.

Church (Rock) Cemetery in Nottingham, looking north, early 1900s. Church Cemetery or Rock Cemetery was designed by Edwin Patchitt, a local solicitor and clerk to the Cemetery Company. The cemetery was created between 1851 and 1856 and was not fully complete when it was opened in 1856. The City Council took over responsibility for the cemetery in 1965 and it remains in their ownership.

Above: General Cemetery, Nottingham, 2011. The General Cemetery seen here was set up by the Nottingham General Cemetery Company. It was established by a special Act of Parliament for which Royal Assent was given on 9 May 1836 and comprised of 14 acres. The Nottingham Enclosure Act provided for the addition of more land to the lower eastern side of the cemetery, and a new entrance lodge and chapel for Dissenters were built. The General Cemetery now covered a total of 18 acres. By 1923, over 150,000 people had been buried on the site. The cemetery quickly deteriorated. In 1955, a Cemetery Action Committee was formed to save the cemetery from further dereliction. The following year, the Crown passed responsibility for the cemetery to Nottingham Corporation.

Opposite above: St Mary's church, the Lace Market, Nottingham. St Mary's is the oldest church in Nottingham. It is quite possible that there was a Saxon church that stood roughly where the present church is. In 1086, a church was mentioned in the Domesday Survey. It was clearly a royal church, described as 'within the King's lordship' with about 75 acres of land, extensive property giving a good income and a priest named Aitard. Most of the church you can see today has been altered and rebuilt many times over its long history. Major alterations were made to the church in the nineteenth century. The church was closed for five years from 1843 to 1848 to allow for the work. The four piers of the tower were rebuilt. The nave and chancel roof timbers and the tracery in the nave clerestory were replaced. The classical west front, which had never been popular, was replaced with a design more like the original.

Right: A fairly gruesome artist's impression, depicting the 'Body Snatchers of Barker Gate'. The industrial expansion of Nottingham's industries in the eighteenth and nineteenth centuries brought with it many problems, not least of which was where to bury the dead. Between 1742 and 1813 three new cemeteries were created on land around Barker Gate. Known officially as Burial Ground No. 1 – Middle Bury – the first of these was consecrated in 1742. Burial Ground No. 2 – Top Bury – was consecrated in 1786, and Burial Ground No. 3 – Bottom Bury – in 1813. The Barker Gate Burial Ground went through a particularly notorious period when graves were plundered for the bodies of the recently buried, by individuals known as 'resurrectionists' or 'resurrection men'. The cadavers were then sold to medical schools for the new medics to hone their anatomical and surgical skills.

St. Peter's Square Nottingham.

Above: St Peter's church, Nottingham, 1890s.
St Peter's church located on St Peter's Gate, is a
church with tower and spire dating to the medieval
period. The early church was presumably a simple
building with a nave and a round apse. It was
destroyed – perhaps twice – in the mid-twelfth
century. In 1140, the army of the Empress Matilda,
attacking the castle held by King Stephen, set fire
to the town and massacred the parishioners of St
Peter's who had taken refuge in the church. The
current church is a rebuild of an earlier church
founded in the early twelfth century. William
Peverel granted land for the building of the church
between 1103 and 1108; it is likely that work
commenced soon after.

Left: St Nicholas also showing St Nicholas' church
walk. The original church on the site was there
around 1100. It was destroyed in 1643 by the
Parliamentarians after being used by the Royalists
to bombard the castle. It was rebuilt in the 1670s
of brick and is the only late seventeenth-century
church in the city. During the development of
Maid Marian Way many of the church burials
were removed for the new road. Also removed for
the development was St Nicholas' church walk,
which can be seen in the image.

ST BARNABAS CATHEDRAL, NOTTINGHAM

Above: The Cathedral Church of St Barnabas, located on the corner of Derby Road and North Circus Street, on the opposite side of which are the Albert Hall and the Nottingham Playhouse. Nottingham's only cathedral was built between 1841 and 1844, costing £15,000, and was first consecrated in 1844. The architect for the cathedral was Augustus Welby Northmore Pugin, who also designed the interior of the Houses of Parliament. It was built in the Early English Plain Gothic style, although in contrast, the Blessed Sacrament chapel was richly decorated and Pugin's later churches were built in that Decorated Gothic style throughout.

Right: Holy Trinity church, Nottingham. The area was renamed Trinity Square after the church was demolished. The church in the Early English style was built on the site in 1839, dedicated to the Holy Trinity. It had a square tower, on which was an octagonal lantern 24 feet high, surmounted with a spire rising 29 feet. The church was demolished in 1958 and the Trinity Square site used for a multistorey car park until 2005. This has now been redeveloped as retail premises.

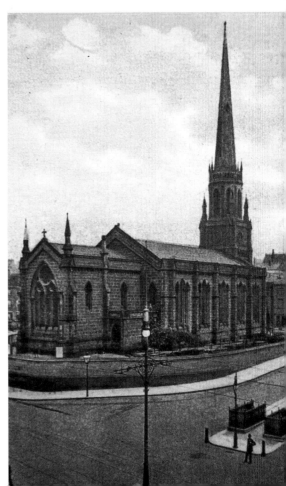

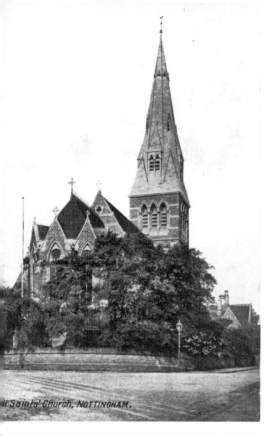

All Saints church, All Saints Street, Nottingham. The original parish of All Saints dates from 1864, a period when the city began to expand and new housing was being rapidly developed. The architect was Thomas Chambers Hine, of Nottingham. The church was consecrated on 3 November 1864; 1,200 people crammed into the 800 seats and there was a large attendance of clergy. At the time of its construction, All Saints' Parish was a new and wealthy suburb outside the old city boundary of Nottingham on an area previously known as Sandfield. The expansion had been as a result of the 1830s cholera epidemic. With the continued expansion of the City of Nottingham, the parish became an inner-city area of Nottingham.

St Andrew's church, Mansfield Road, c. 1902. This church is situated on Mansfield Road, opposite the Church (Rock) Cemetery, on or near the site of the Nottingham Gallows. It was built by William Knight in 1869–71, with a west baptistry added by S. R. Stevenson in 1884 and vestries by Heazell & Sons in 1905. Built of rock-faced Bulwell stone, it comprises a nave of four bays and aisles, a chancel under the tower, a sanctuary, transept chapels, baptistry, north and south porches and a tower with tourelles and with a broach spire, containing one bell by Mears & Stainbank dated 1871.

8

Street Life: North of the City

38 Mansfield Road, Nottingham.

Mansfield Road, looking north from the city, early 1990s. This scene of Mansfield Road, just as it leaves the city centre, has not changed much to this day. One of the most recognisable buildings in the photograph is the Rose of England public house, which can be seen on the right. Originally a hotel, it was built in 1898. The building was designed by one of Nottingam's most respected architects, Watson Fothergill.

Above: Mansfield Road, June 1971. The photograph was taken at the start of Mansfield Road as it leaves the city. Just a few metres up from this area is the Victoria Centre. The Mansfield Arms can be seen to the right. The Mansfield Arms dated back to 1894 and it retained the same name for eighty years. Since 1973 there has been a succession of changes in its title. The building still stands and is currently used as a public house.

Opposite above: Mansfield Road Wesleyan Chapel, Mansfield Road, March 1973. Mansfield Road Wesleyan chapel is being demolished in this picture. The chapel was located on the junction of Mansfield Road and Woodborough Road. The foundation stone for the chapel was laid on 22 May 1871.

Opposite below: Mansfield Road and Bluecoat Street, January 1971. The Mansfield Road and Bluecoat Street can be seen, taken from Woodborough Road. Bluecoat Street can be seen straight ahead leading off from the Mansfield Road. In the very far distance can be seen the Bluecoat Street New church being demolished. Across from the old church is the old site of the Bluecoat School. The building still exists but it is no longer used as a school. The Bluecoat School was founded in 1706 by Timothy Fenton, rector of St Peter's church (1705–21), and the incumbents of the two other Nottingham parishes, St Mary's and St Nicholas'. It was Nottingham's first elementary school which educated both sexes free of charge. It took its name from the blue uniforms provided for the pupils.

Parliament Street, *c.* 1890, looking east towards the junction with Milton Street showing The Unicorn pub on the far left and The Milton's Head Hotel in the top right. The hotel and the pub were both demolished in the late 1960s to make way for the then new Victoria Shopping Centre. Both the hotel and pub would have roughly stood where the main entrance to the Victoria Centre is today.

Lower Parliament Street, *c.* 1898. The Original Dog & Partridge public house can be seem to the left, Bass & Wilford Chemist in the centre and Newcastle Street can be seen on the right. In the 1898 *Wright's Directory*, Albert Freeman is listed as the licensee of The Original Dog & Partridge.

Milton Street, *c.* 1905, looking north from its junction with Parliament Street. The corner of the Milton's Head Hotel can be seen on the right. In the distance to the left can be seen the Mechanic's Institute and Holy Trinity church.

Milton Street, *c.* 1910, looking west from Victoria station. The large building to the left of the photograph is the original Mechanic's Institute. The institute has been a centre of social, educational and cultural activities in the city since 1837. The 'Nottingham Mechanics' is one of the only few left in the country that still survives from its Victorian beginnings.

Derby Road, Nottingham, early 1900s. Image taken from Canning Circus looking down Derby Road. On the left can be seen Wollaton Street. The building in the middle was originally a Boots store. It was later occupied by Ben Bowers restaurant.

J. Chadbourne,

70 Derby Road,

NOTTINGHAM.

Perambulator Manufacturer.

After 40 years' experience in the Pram Trade I have every confidence in submitting my list, which can be had on application.

All the Carriages are built on the premises, under my personal supervision, and are Guaranteed of the Best Workmanship and Material.

Therefore our Prices are Moderate owing to our own production and Strictly Cash Transactions.

Repairs a Speciality.

TELEPHONE 5092.

An old advert for J. Chadbourne, 70 Derby Road, Nottingham.

Above: Chapel Bar, Nottingham, early nineteenth century. An early nineteenth-century artist's impression of the view taken from Chapel Bar looking down into Nottingham's Market Place. Chapel Bar was the old west gate into the walled enclosure of Nottingham and was erected possibly sometime in the thirteenth century.

Inset: Chapel Bar, Nottingham, seventeenth century. In Nottingham any thoroughfare with 'Bar' in its name denotes one that would bar or block your passage at some point or time – as in a Toll Bar, a point where you would have to pay to continue along that route. Any thoroughfare with 'Gate' in its name denotes 'Place' or 'Place of' from the Old Norse *gata* (path). Originally Bar Gate, the place of the bar, and the site one of the town gates. When this gate went out of use, one of the drum towers was converted into a small chapel for passing travellers. This was the catalyst for the name change to 'Chapel Bar' at a later time.

Canning Circus, Nottingham, 1880s. A cab shelter and water trough can be seen in the centre on Alfreton Road, Canning Circus. At the back can be seen the terrace and the old almshouses. The terrace is the gatehouse to the General Cemetery and was built for this purpose. It is flanked by Almshouses (listed Grade II), and was designed by S. S. Rawlinson for the General Cemetery Company. Built between 1837 and 1840 in stucco and brick, it has slate roofs and corniced stacks.

Talbot Street, Nottingham, 1926. Mounted police can be seen on Talbot Street in Nottingham. Established before the invention of motor cars, mounted police were important for the safety and protection of the public on all roads and public open spaces.

Above: The interior of the now demolished 'Central Market', which was located on King Edward Street, 1938. The Central Market opened at this site on 21 November 1928, having relocated from Market Square; the market itself would relocate once again to a section of the newly constructed Victoria Shopping Centre in the early 1970s.

Opposite above: Demolition of houses in Stratford Square off Shakespeare Street, 12 March 1967.

Opposite below: St Ann's Street, Nottingham, 1930s, showing Geo Shipman Newsagents, the White Hart Inn and Foresters Arms public. Glasshouse Street can be seen to the right of the photograph.

A view of King Edward Street, taken from a trolley bus, early 1960s. Nottingham residents have many fond memories of the trolley buses in the city. The Nottingham trolleybus system opened on 10 April 1927. It gradually replaced the Nottingham tramway network. The Nottingham system was a medium-sized one, with a total of eight routes, and a maximum fleet of 157 trolleybuses. It was closed on 30 June 1966.

Street Life: South of the City

Park Valley, the Park Estate, Nottingham, *c.* 1900. The Park Estate is a private residential housing estate to the west of Nottingham city centre. It was built on the former deer park of Nottingham Castle. The area of the Park Estate covers some 150 acres. It was designed by the pre-eminent architect Thomas Chambers Hine for the 5th Duke of Newcastle as a quality residential estate in the early 1850s.

PARK STEPS, NOTTINGHAM.

The Park Steps, The Park Estate, Nottingham, early 1900s. The Park Steps are located to the north side of the Park Estate in Nottingham. The steps were probably cut into an existing slopping track in the late 1820s when access to the first houses in what became Park Valley was needed. They have been continually upgraded since the early 1830s.

OFFICES TO LET

Bridlesmith Gate, Nottingham, looking south. The view looks down Bridlesmith Gate towards Low Pavement and Drury Hill. The name of Bridlesmith is very old. It was called Bridlesmith Gate (or something very like it) as long ago as 1304 and it reflects something of the importance of the smiths of Nottingham. A 'Bridlesmith' was a maker of snaffles, bits, stirrups and other horse, saddle and harness furniture.

Above: Wheeler Gate, Nottingham, *c.* 1916. The real name for Wheeler Gate in Nottingham should really be Wheel Wright Gate, meaning, the street where the wheel makers lived. In earlier times it had another name, for in 1313 it is referred to as Baxter Gate, and it is quite possible that the Baxter House or bake house of the town was situated hereabouts during the fourteenth century.

Right: Hounds Gate, Nottingham, *c.* 1920. View looking up Hounds Gate towards St Peter's church. J. Holland Walker in *The Transactions of the Thoroton Society* (1928), describes Hounds Gate as having 'extreme antiquity, being a section of the earliest primeval track in this neighbourhood'. In 1326, it was known as Hungate. Walker describes Hounds Gate as 'being an important thoroughfare throughout the Middle Ages, linking the Castle with the town'.

Above: View looking towards Exchange Walk, 1950s. Exchange Walk was made in 1868. It was originally a yard which went by the name of Gears' Yard, after a certain William Gears who occupied it and who was a fishmonger in Nottingham Market Place. Then its name was changed to Farmer's Yard after James Farmer who established the drapery business upon its western side. James Farmer and the authorities of Smith's Bank saw the great benefit that would accrue to the town and to themselves by forming a thoroughfare from St Peter's Square to the Market Place, so at their joint expense they made Exchange Walk.

Opposite above: Castle Gate, Nottingham, 1945. Walker (1929) in his *An itinerary of Nottingham*, describes Castle Gate as 'the most beautiful and dignified street in the whole city. Its splendid Georgian houses with their beautiful details and exquisite brickwork, the historical associations of many of its houses and above all the great balloon of the chestnut tree which peeps out from St Nicholas Churchyard render it a perfect delight to walk up. It is not a very old street, as streets go in Nottingham, and is first mentioned in 1315. Its early name was French Gate which shows it to have been constructed in connection with the new town formed soon after the Conquest.'

Opposite below: Lister Gate, Nottingham, 1950s, looking north towards Market Square. Lister Gate is an old thoroughfare going back as far as 1303, when it was referred to as 'Litster Gate' or Dyers Street. The dyers no doubt congregated here in order to make use of the waters of the River Leen.

Walter Fountain, Lister Gate, *c.* 1900. The Walter Fountain was designed by a Mr Sutton in a Victorian Gothic style in 1866 and commissioned by Mr John Walter, son of John Walter of Bear-Wood, at a cost of £1,000. It was demolished in the 1950s when the road was widened. It was located at the junction of Greyfriar Gate, Lister Gate and Carrington Street.

Left: Drury Hill, Nottingham, 1906. Drury Hill was a medieval narrow lane. It was only 4 feet 10 inches wide at its narrowest point. The old name for Drury Hill was Vault Lane, which became Parkyn Lane, probably after some member of the Parkyn family of Bunny who lived there, and eventually it was changed into Drury Hill, around 1620. Jackson's can be seen on the left and Danby on the right. All of these buildings have now gone. Drury Hill and all of the surrounding area was sadly demolished in the 1960s to make way for the Broad Marsh Shopping Centre.

Below: Lister Gate, Nottingham, late 1800s. A very early photograph of Lister Gate, looking north towards St Peter's Square. The Walter Fountain can be seen to the left of the photograph.

Drury Hill, Nottingham, 1940s. Despite the protests by many Nottingham residents, they failed in their bid to stop Drury Hill being demolished in the 1960s to make way for the entrance to the then new Broad Marsh Shopping Centre. With its narrowness and congestion, and its curious haphazard buildings, Drury Hill gives us some idea of the appearance of what medieval Nottingham would have looked like.

Middle Hill, looking from Garner's Hill. Middle Hill, which was known as Mont Hall Hill
– derived from Mont Hall, 'The Hall upon the Hill', named after the old Guildhall – was an
unusual looking building which stood at the top of the hill in Weekday Cross till the end of
the nineteenth century. Another interesting curio regarding Middle Hill concerns a man called
Bamford, who lived upon Middle Hill around 1825. He was one of the last men in Nottingham
who kept a Sedan Chair for hire.

Garner's Hill, Nottingham, late 1800s. Garner's Hill was one of the ancient southern entrances into the city. It was sadly demolished in 2006 to make way for the Nottingham Contemporary. Garner's Hill with its steps was a branch of the same thoroughfare that formed Middle Hill. It was formerly called Brightmore's Hill, apparently after a certain William Brightmore who in the early part of the seventeenth century was something of a 'divine' and wrote a paraphrase of the Book of Revelation.

The site of Garner's Hill, June 2006. The old site of Garner's Hill can be seen being demolished and redeveloped to make way for the Nottingham Contemporary Art Gallery.

Above: The old railway tunnel, Garner's Hill, June 2006. This shows the old site of Garner's Hill being demolished and redeveloped for the Nottingham Contemporary. The tunnel led to the Victoria station under Thurland Street and was the Great Central Railway line. The area is now covered over by modern tram tracks and the Nottingham Contemporary Art Gallery.

Opposite: Red Lion Street, Narrow Marsh, *c.* 1913. Nottingham was founded on a sandstone outcrop, below which to the south were flood meadows towards the River Trent. St Mary's church was established on the eastern end of this outcrop, and the Saxon town developed here. In the eleventh century, the Normans built a castle on the western side. To aid the defence of this castle, they diverted the River Leen to flow below the Castle Rock, and from there it continued in an easterly direction, before turning south to meet the River Trent. It flowed below the eastern end of the town, leaving marshy ground between it and the sandstone rock. The western and wider area was called Broad Marsh, and the narrowest part, Narrow Marsh. The River Leen yet again became diverted, so areas like Broad Marsh and Narrow Marsh were therefore freed from flooding problems and they were eventually built on. A large part of the area later became known as Red Lion Street, after the eponymous public house.

Above: Cliff Street – High Pavement, Narrow Marsh, early 1900s. By the nineteenth and twentieth centuries, Nottingham's population was rapidly expanding. In the sixteenth century the population probably never exceeded 3,000 people. Then it started to increase – by 1750 it was about 10,000 in the first census of 1801 it was almost 29,000 and by 1841 it was over 50,000, packed into almost the same area as that of the medieval town. One of the worst slum areas in Nottingham was Narrow Marsh, the overcrowding led to the appalling yards and alleys of the area. Narrow Marsh quickly became notorious for its crime, poverty and slums. By the 1920s and '30s, nearly all of Narrow Marsh was demolished and the inhabitants moved to new Corporation housing estates.

Opposite below: Warser Gate, Nottingham, 2005, looking west along Warser Gate. The area around Warser Gate was redeveloped in 2005. New apartments can be seen being built in the centre of the photograph. The building to the middle left of the photograph is the Adam's Building, which was restored and converted in 1996 for a new college campus by New College Nottingham.

Short Hill, the Lace Market, Nottingham, 1960. Short Hill is still very much the same as it was in the Georgian period. The Georgian houses along Short Hill are very notable. Walker (1927) describes 'the houses upon Short Hill above [as] very interesting. First of all, there is a XVII century house at the eastern end which always looks to me as if it ought to have a very interesting story, but that story has eluded me, and beyond the fact that during the XVII century it was used as a school. In front of it was a public well which was filled up long ago. The houses facing Hollowstone (numbers 1 and 2) have plain and dignified eighteenth century doorways with good fanlights, and inside are excellent staircases. The most dramatic resident upon Short Hill was Sir William Parsons, Baronet, whose son William was executed at Tyburn in 1751. This lad had a terrible history. He became a highwayman, and eventually was recognised as an escaped convict and condemned to death, and later was hanged as a malefactor upon the public gallows at Tyburn.'

Above: Goose Gate, Nottingham, 1960/'70s. Goose Gate, which, together with Hockley, formed the ancient Walker Gate, gets its name from Robert-le-Gos, who was a goldsmith living here around 1300. He was a man of considerable importance in his generation, and was elected Bailiff no fewer than eight times. Across the road in the middle of the photograph can be seen Gillotts. Gillotts was a hardware store on Goose Gate.

Previous page: Pelham Street, Nottingham, April 1971. Pelham Street is a fairly modern name for a very ancient thoroughfare. Before it was known as Pelham Street, it was called Gridlesmith Gate or sometimes Girdlesmith Gate. Gridlesmiths made pot hooks, pot cranes and other pieces of fireplace furniture; they degraded later to plowshares nails and other farm related metal items. In its heyday, the smiths of Nottingham were held in high esteem, as an oft told saying goes: 'the little smith of Nottingham that makes the things that no man can.' After the clearing away of these assorted gridlesmiths and widening – with funds donated by one of the Pelham family – thus the road was renamed Pelham Street.

10

Street Life: The Outskirts of the City

Sneinton Market, Sneinton, Nottingham, early 1900s. Sneinton is a south-eastern suburb of Nottingham. In 1801, the population of Sneinton stood at just 588. Sneinton was then no more than a village about a mile outside of Nottingham town centre, standing on a high ridge overlooking the valley of the River Trent. Within just fifty years, however, the population had grown to 8,440. With the population continuing to rise, Sneinton was officially incorporated into the borough of Nottingham in 1877.

Above: An eighteenth-century artist's impression of the Shepherd's Race, or Robin Hood's Race, Sneinton, Nottingham. The Shepherd's Race was cut into flat ground near the summit of Blue Bell Hill — Thorneywood Mount — in the St Ann's district of Nottingham. The hill was part of Sneinton Common, given to the parish as 'common land' by the Pierrepont family. It is described as being 34–35 yards across, covering an area of 324 square yards, with a single path 535 yards long. These proportions make the race one of the largest examples of its kind. Its design is fairly typical of the medieval kind, with the addition of four rounded extensions or bastions. Each enclosed a small mound with a design known in heraldry as a 'cross-crosslet' cut into the top. The bastions are said to have aligned with the four cardinal points of the compass.

Inset: Monks 'treading' the Shepherd's Race, Sneinton, Nottingham. A charming, if inaccurate, illustration of kneeling monks on the turf path of the maze. The origin of the Shepherd's Race, as with most mazes, is speculative. One modern author on the subject states that the maze was cut in the fourth century and modified by the Templar Knights for use in their rituals. Two eighteenth-century antiquarians pass comment on the maze. William Stukeley delivers a popular opinion of the time when he declares it to be 'of Roman origin'. Charles Deering says, 'It seems to be a name of no old standing.' He disputes Stukeley's opinion and declares, 'It is evidently, from the cross-crosslets in the centres of the four lesser rounds, and in that there are no banks raised but circular trenches cut into the turf, and those so narrow that persons cannot run in them, but must run on top of the turf, it is of no Roman origin and yet is more ancient than the reformation.'

Opposite: Green's Windmill, Sneinton, Nottingham, 2005. Green's Windmill in Sneinton was built by the father of notable scientist and mathematician George Green in 1807. The mill was badly damaged by a fire in 1947, but was later restored by Nottingham City Council in the 1980s. The windmill began milling again in December 1986 and the giant sails can still be seen working to this day. George Green was a mathematical genius who developed new ways of doing mathematics, which have since helped generations of scientists with their research and work.

Above: St Ann's Well Road during demolition, St Ann's, Nottingham, early 1970s. By the nineteenth century, Nottingham was populated mainly by lace and textile workers, who needed houses. St Ann's was an obvious location, with the street plan based on three major roads running north-eastwards: St Ann's Well Road, Blue Bell Hill Road and Carlton Road. Factories, workshops and other industrial buildings were built alongside the houses so that workers did not have far to travel. By the end of the nineteenth century, the whole area was virtually filled with high-density housing. 10,000 houses were packed into St Ann's by 1890s and two-thirds of them had no hot water and three quarters no bath. In the late 1960s and early 1970s, Nottingham Council decided to demolish most of the old nineteenth-century houses, to be replaced by more modern homes. Much of the area was rebuilt during the 1970s and 1980s, often with new street patterns. Many local residents were moved out to other areas of the city and their close communities split up.

Opposite above: St Ann's Well Tram Terminus, Coppice Road, St Ann's, Nottingham, early 1900s. Coppice Road was built as a thoroughfare in 1837 connecting Coppice Lodge to Mapperley Plain with tollgates at each end. It ran through the Coppice and was later renamed Ransom Road.

Opposite below: St Ann's Well, St Anns, Nottingham, 1860. The earliest written reference to the St Ann's Well gives the name as Brodwell – possibly derived from the Saxon Brod, a coming together or to shoot or spout. This name was still in use as late as 1301. An alternative name occurring in written references is Owswell. In 1216, an event took place that was to set the Well on its course in history. In this year, elders of the town met with King Henry III to ask for a repeal of certain Forest Laws to the benefit of the starving poor. Deer in the forest were culled twice a year and it was decided that the product of the spring cull was to be used for the benefit of the town. The cull in the area around the Well was arranged to take place at the time of the Festival of Easter. It was made compulsory for all the 'town people' to attend at the well for a great feast followed by the distribution of meat. Thus began the annual pilgrimage to the Well on Easter Monday.

St Ann's Well site, St Ann's, Nottingham, 1987. In 1987, the site of the St Ann's Well was believed to have been discovered in the Gardener's Public House car park. This site was privately excavated by Mr David Greenwood and the results subsequently published in 2007 in *Robin of St Ann's Well Road*. Here David Greenwoood (on the right) and Paul Nix from the Nottingham Hidden History Team (on the left) can be seen during the excavation period of the well.

Arkwright Street Floods, The Meadows, Nottingham, March 1947. The flooding resulted from exceptionally cold weather which swept in from Russia bringing snow and frost. As the snows melted, the River Trent burst its banks at Wilford and West Bridgford, the floodwaters reaching as far north as Nottingham Midland Railway station. The harsh weather came at a particularly bad time after the Second World War, when people were still suffering rationing, and caused severe hardship for many.

Old Wilford, Nottingham. A very countrified-looking Wilford can be seen before it really became developed in the nineteenth and twentieth centuries. Wilford is a village close to the centre of the city of Nottingham. The village is bound to the north and west by the River Trent. Wilford retained its identity as a village until the later nineteenth century. Surrounded by woodlands and with riverside amenities such as the Wilford Ferry Inn, the village attracted many visitors from Nottingham. Spencer Hall, the Nottinghamshire poet, wrote in 1846, 'Who ever saw Wilford without wishing to become an inmate of one of its peaceful woodbined homes.'

11

Nottingham Caves

Members of the Nottingham Hidden History Team (NHHT) and the Nottingham Historical & Archaeological Society (NHAS) can be seen hard at work around the late 1970s. During the 1960s and '70s, the NHHT recorded, cleaned and helped preserve many cave sites that would otherwise have been lost forever. In the 1960s and 1970s, the team found themselves involved with various cave explorations. It was groups like the NHHT and NHAS who were the first 'generation' of archaeological groups to record and preserve the caves for future prosperity.

Above: Caves under the Flying Horse Hotel, Nottingham, late 1970s. Members of the NHAS and the NHHT can be seen recording and excavating the caves under the Flying Horse Hotel, South Parade in Nottingham's Old Market Square. In the 1960s and '70s, groups such as these recorded a lot of Nottingham's caves before they were destroyed and lost forever by the developments in the city of those decades.

Opposite: Paul Nix from the NHHT under Long Row, Market Square, Nottingham, 1982. Paul Nix, founder and Team Leader of the NHHT, can be seen photographed in the caves under Long Row. The original NHHT was formed in 1965. The purpose of the team was to try to save, or at least record before destruction, the cave sites continually discovered during the major redevelopment of the city in the 1960s and onwards. Almost every day, new sites were unearthed and destroyed before anyone was officially notified; the last thing contractors wanted was someone telling them to stop work on a project. 'Time is money' as they say, so the team had to work quickly and sometimes under pressure to record the caves before they were lost forever in some cases.

Above: Caves under the Flying Horse Hotel, Nottingham, late 1970s. The two levels of rock-cut beer cellars of The Flying Horse Hotel are connected by a wide (around 2½-metre width) tunnel. The Flying Horse Hotel is a former public house dating back to the fifteenth century. Before being built, it was the site of the house that the Plumptre family erected for themselves when they first came to Nottingham in the thirteenth century. As such, some of the caves under there could well date to that period or even earlier.

Left: Caves under Goose Gate, Nottingham, January 1979. At this time, shops along Goose Gate were being demolished. While the land was being levelled, it was decided to excavate the site before further development. On 30 January 1979, while scraping a section around 20 yards in from Goosegate, a large hole was found containing an opening into a cave system. Paul Nix and members of the Nottingham Hidden History Team were called in to excavate and record the caves.

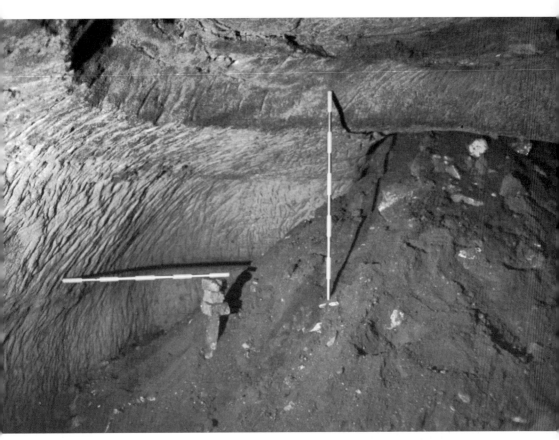

Caves under Goose Gate, Nottingham, January 1979. The caves under Goose Gate were recorded and excavated by the NHHT over a period of a week. Through their work, it was discovered that the cave system was Nottingham's first brewery (called Simpson's), on land leased from Richard Arkwright. It was also found that part of the system was an underground slaughterhouse used by a pork butcher's shop, which over several years had various uses. By the end of the NHHT's dig, the Council's Department of Technical Services decided to save the caves and preserve them.

Left: Daniel in the Lion's Den Lions, Bottom Cave, The Park Estate, Nottingham, 1984. The name of this cave, Daniel in the Lion's Den, is purely because of the large carving to the rear of the main chamber. This has to be one of the finest cave carvings in Nottingham, and is located inside a cave cut into the sandstone escarpment overlooking The Park Estate from the north-east. The cave carving represents Daniel and six lions, and to give you an idea of its size the whole carving must be in the region of some 15–18 feet (4.5 metres to 5.4 metres) high. The lions measure 6 feet (1.8 metres) from the head to the base of the tail. Daniel himself measures 6 feet (1.8 metres) from shoulder to knee. So, as we can see, these are one and a half times lifesize.

W. H. S. Colonnade, Cave Pillars, The Park Estate, Nottingham, 1984. In a cliff face, on a garden terrace that connected through a tunnel to the rear of a house on The Ropewalk, is a cave called the Colonnade. The Colonnade is a rectangular chamber, 5 metres wide at the cliff face and extending into the cliff for 9 metres. Inside the chamber there are three parallel rows of six pillars each, which are all free-standing, connected only to the floor and ceiling. The height of the ceiling is 2.5 metres and is mostly level. All the pillars measure approximately 35 cm across, but some are worn and one has had bricks put around it. The entrance to the cave is through a very large doorway with another pillar in the centre of it. From this entrance to the back of the cave, the floor is covered in bricks laid flat and at the far end a series of steps leads us up to the bricked-up passageway entrance.

Opposite below: Daniel in the Lion's Den, Bottom Cave, The Park Estate, Nottingham, 1984. As well as the Daniel in the Lion's Den carvings, the same room features a buttress, three feet (90 centimetres) wide, followed by another archway some 5 feet (1.5 metres) wide. At the top of the buttress, an hourglass is carved in the rock. Another buttress of 1 foot (30 cm) is followed by an archway of 4 feet (1.2 metres) at the top of which a large face is carved with its mouth open, investigation showed it was designed to be an air vent. Looking across to the opposite wall there is a blank section from the front window to the doorway into the long passage. On this wall was another shield with the initials of its constructor, Alderman Thomas Herbett. On the opposite side of the doorway, there is a 1 foot (30 centimetres) wide pillar followed by another arch. Just after the arch, there is a large chunk of rock wall, which has been brick-faced and was not too secure. It is quite obvious from the constructional details of this system that it was finished to a very high standard. Alas, time and the elements have done their bit to destroy this creation, one of the rear legs of the lion at the bottom has fallen off, and a lot of carvings that are in close proximity to the main entrance and windows have suffered from the weather and, in recent times, vandals. The carving has since been protected by adding doors and shutters to protect it from weathering and vandalism.

W. H. S. Colonnade, Crucifix Cave Carving, The Park Estate, Nottingham, 1984. Looking down the left-hand wall of the colonnade there are six niches, each of which has a carved statue. Most of these are very worn, partially due to the nature of the rock from which they are cut. This crucifix carving has survived well and illustrates the fine detail of the carvings. Bunter sandstone carvings do not fare well in exposed or draughty positions. These carvings have also had many hands on them over the years. At least two of the statues are quite unrecognisable.